C000270169

GREAT GOLF HOLES
OF IRELAND

Photographs were supplied courtesy of the parties listed below :
Bord Failte : Holes 4, 10, 12, 14, 18.
Northern Ireland Tourist Board : Holes 7, 9.
Christopher Hill Photographic : Cover + holes 2, 3, 13, 15, 17.
The Slide File Ltd : Holes 1, 5, 6, 8, 11, 16.

Illustrations by Richard Irons.

Design & Production by Mitchell Kane Associates.

Thanks to Peter and Gordon Welsh for their help and good ideas

Special thanks to Catherine Coyle for her support.

Printed in Northern Ireland by The Universities Press (Belfast) Ltd.

Published by Causeway Press (N.I.), Enterprise House, Balloo Avenue, Bangor, Northern Ireland BT19 2QT.
Telephone (0247) 271525. Fax (0247) 270080.

GREAT GOLF HOLES
OF IRELAND

compiled by

Paul Slevin

with a foreword by

Christy O' Connor

INDEX

FOREWORD

In the 47 years that I have been a professional golfer, I have played all round the world and taken part in many Ryder Cup campaigns, but I have no hesitation in saying that the holes selected for this book are among the most demanding that I have ever seen.

They will test more than just the clubs in your bag. Your mental strength, physical stamina, and even your head for heights will all come under close examination.

Ireland offers not only some of the greatest golf courses in the world but also the scenery to match. As a test of golf, these holes certainly ask some very tough questions, but the player can at least enjoy the spectacular views while searching for the answers.

Christy O'Connor

WHITE ROCKS GOLF CLUB
1st : ARCHERY
176 yards par 3

The links at White Rocks are undergoing constant change, brought about by the destructive effect of the sea on the spectacular chalk cliffs that make up this part of the Antrim Coast.

In effect, parts of the course have become something of a geological sculpture park, and some of the work on show is quite stunning, as we can see in this view from the tee on Archery, one of four pitch holes on the course.

The key to playing the hole is to hit the green with your tee shot - no matter how you do it. Should you miss, you will probably be playing your second from the beach below. Faced with this almost impossible sand shot, it is always good advice to abandon your first attempt and play a second ball from the tee.

Indeed, this is such standard practice that, on one occasion, when a player who had missed the green demanded a sand wedge, he had to wait for nearly ten minutes before his caddie returned with a ham and cheese roll.

Difficult as the beach shot is, however, the club professional insists that the toughest shot on this hole is to drill the ball hard, low, and to the right so that it rebounds off one of the bridge posts, hurdles the bunker, and rolls up the green and into the hole. The shot is so difficult, apparently, that he has managed it only once.

CONNEMARA GOLF CLUB
2ND : PONY TREK
147 yards par 3

Connemara provides a stiff challenge for even the most inventive of golf course architects. The area is comprised mainly of bogland punctuated by bare rock, yet these features have been incorporated successfully into many of the local courses.

Pony Trek is a classic example. The hole sits on top of an unusual rock formation, shaped only in part by the elements. Animals, rather than the weather, are responsible for the deep cuts in the rock-face which have been gouged out by the hooves of hundreds of generations of Connemara ponies, bag carriers to local golfers before the advent of caddies.

Many of the older members insist that they received far better advice from the horse's mouth than they have ever had from a caddie. The main drawback of the ponies, unfortunately, was their tendency to eat more grass than the average caddie, resulting in the erosion that remains evident today.

Despite the harshness of the terrain, the ultimate test on Pony Trek is not to find the green with your tee shot, but to stay on it. Although the grass is kept a little longer in order to slow the pace of the green, it is still considered generous to concede even the fourth or fifth putt in a matchplay situation.

When it comes to holing out, it is worth remembering that Conne-mara is the largest of the *Gaeltacht*, or Gaelic-speaking, areas in Ireland, and it may be to your advantage, therefore, if you can read your putts in Irish.

DUNLUCE CASTLE GOLF CLUB
3rd : TINKER'S SEAT
195 yards par 3

The Tinker's Seat is the opening hole on these famous links. The tee-off clings to the rockface in the shadow of the original clubhouse which dates back to around the year 1300.

The most remarkable event in the club's history was also a tragic one. The clubhouse paid the price for its precarious position when the kitchen, along with catering staff who were preparing dinner at the time, fell into the sea in 1639. The bar was fortunate enough to survive, although, from that day to this, members have refrained from adding water to their whiskey, and it is certainly frowned upon to ask for 'one on the rocks'.

A visiting tinker, who was sitting on an adjacent window ledge, had a lucky escape as he watched the kitchen disappear over the edge of the cliff. The clubhouse was abandoned two years later due to the lack of catering facilities, but the Tinker's Window, as it is now known, can still be seen today.

The Tinker's Seat is a notoriously difficult opening hole - as water hazards go, few can be more daunting than the Atlantic Ocean. Since all golfers recognise the importance of a good start to the round, there is always strong demand for starting times which coincide with a low tide. As a result, many a round must finish by the light of the moon.

BERE ISLAND GOLF CLUB
4th : BEACH LANDING
452 yards par 4

Although Bere Island can be found just off the coast of Cork, locals maintain that the course was developed from land owned by a farmer from Kerry who was awarded a Nobel prize for being out standing in his field.

As the visitor to this area will quickly come to realise, talking can have a very important influence on the outcome of a golf match in the county of Cork.

It pays to beware of blarney, especially as it originated in these parts. The locals' gift of the gab can be traced back to Cormac McCarthy, Lord of Blarney, and supposedly loyal subject of Queen Elizabeth I who was colonising Ireland at the time. He was notorious for failing to fulfil his agreements with the Queen : it was said that he could "talk the noose off his neck". To this day, anyone kissing the Blarney stone at Blarney castle is said to be similarly endowed with the gift of eloquent and persuasive speech.

As a result, unwary visitors have been known to concede putts of anything up to ten feet to locals who have kissed the stone. When it comes to cutting the corner on Beach Landing, others have been persuaded to bite off more than they can chew. Although the fairway on this hole turns at a perfect right angle, legend has it that even the great Pythagoras was talked into having a go for the green despite the fact that it requires a carry of almost 350 yards.

LAKES OF KILLARNEY GOLF CLUB
5th : CENTURY
235 yards par 3

Water is never far away on this lake-strewn course, but Century perhaps has more than its fair share. The waterfall is supplied from a body of water known locally as the Devil's Punchbowl whih dispenses its contents through a narrow channel called the Devil's Stream before it cascades down the side of Mangerton Mountain.

Both the green and the men's tee are reached by a series of stepping stones which can become submerged after a period of heavy rain. During the wet winter months, the hole can only be played from the safety of the ladies' tee which has direct access to dry land.

The most celebrated attempt to play the hole took place during Captain's Day in 1895, a time when golfballs were stuffed with feathers. Competition was fierce that day, but favourite for the prize was Major Patrick Flanagan, the finest player in the club at that time but a very stubborn individual.

Flanagan was furious with himself when his tee shot to Cascade missed the green and was carried back down the mountain. On seeing the ball float past the tee, he instructed his caddie to purloin a rowing boat which was tied up nearby, and they both set off in pursuit, Flanagan swinging wildly at the floating ball as the caddie manned the oars.

The ball finally reached dry land almost half a mile downstream. Flanagan, not one to give up easily, elected to play through the forest and eventually found the green, holing out in exactly one hundred strokes. His endeavours, however, were ultimately rewarded with first prize when it emerged that nobody else had managed to complete the hole that day.

DOOEGA HEAD GOLF CLUB
6th : ATLANTIC DRIVE
527 yards par 5

Dooega Head can be found on Achill Island, just off the coast of Mayo. This course is not for the fair weather golfer but the members, who are made of sterner stuff, enjoy the challenge of a few holes over its tough links, no matter what the elements may throw at them.

Although Mayo is not renowned for being the sunniest part of Ireland, temperatures during the hot summer of 1976 reached an uncomfortable 85 degrees Fahrenheit in the shade - while listening to a weather report at the time, one member expressed his relief that he did not have to play in the shade.

Atlantic Drive is not particularly long for a par five, but even the big hitters usually take three good ones to get up in two. The hole is fully exposed to the prevailing winds that sweep in from the Atlantic Ocean and it pays good dividends, therefore, to keep the ball low into the wind, even when you are putting.

The members have a healthy love-hate relationship with this hole and, over the years, a few have even had their ashes scattered into the sea from the edge of its cliffs. On the last occasion that such a ceremony took place, a large gust of wind came along at the vital moment and blew the ashes inland. The captain was heard to remark that it was the first time the deceased had actually hit the fairway on Atlantic Drive.

SKELLIG GOLF CLUB
7th : SAINT MICHAEL'S VIEW
424 yards par 4

Saint Michael's View is one of only nine holes on this mountainous course which clings to a rocky outcrop, just off the Kerry coastline, known as Great Skellig or Skellig Michael.

The island is dedicated to Saint Michael, guardian against the power of darkness and patron of high places. On reaching it by boat, visitors are greeted by a steep climb up the ancient stone steps to the ruins of Saint Finian's Abbey which was established by monks back in 560 AD.

The other island in view is Little Skellig which is uninhabited except for thousands of sea birds that enjoy sanctuary there.

A prayer to Saint Michael or Saint Finian may be a good idea before driving off on Saint Michael's View. The sloping fairway and thick rough make it a very difficult hole if you are not on top of your game. It is often said that the best way to play it is under an assumed name.

The hole is occasionally birdied, but members back in the bar were filled with disbelief when word filtered in from the course that somebody had scored an albatross (three under par!). The albatross, as it turned out, had been killed in mid-flight to the sanctuary on Little Skellig by an errant golf ball. The bird was later stuffed and mounted above the bar as a constant reminder of how much a story can change in the telling.

CLEW BAY GOLF CLUB
8th : SAINT PATRICK'S TOLL
427 yards par 4

Clew Bay is a truly unique golf course - one that can only be played at low tide, unless you have access to a boat to ferry you between holes. Local enterprise, however, ensures that you can choose from a wide-ranging flotilla of seagoing caddies.

During slow play, it is even possible to combine a bit of fishing with your golf, and the catering staff are usually happy to prepare your catch should you wish to dine at the clubhouse after your round.

Saint Patrick's Toll, which is the opening hole on the course, sits in the shadow of Ireland's holiest mountain, Croagh Patrick. The picture opposite is taken from its summit where Saint Patrick spent the forty days of lent in prayer and fasting in the year 441 AD. A small chapel at the summit marks the spot from where he drove all the snakes out of Ireland, sending them to their doom in Clew Bay.

The exercise was achieved with the aid of a bell which Saint Patrick rang before throwing it repeatedly over the edge of the mountain, each time taking with it a stream of snakes. The bell was spirited back up and the process repeated until the expulsion was complete.

The bell, which is now used to call time in the clubhouse bar, is as popular with the members today as it used to be with the snakes.

CAUSEWAY COAST
GOLF AND COUNTRY CLUB

9th : FINN MacCOOL'S PITCH
268 yards par 4

A short but deceptively difficult par four, this hole is unique in terms of golfing architecture, sitting on top of the world-renowned Giant's Causeway which was built long ago by the Irish giant, Finn MacCool.

Finn built the causeway to bridge the Irish Sea so that he could join combat with the Scottish giant, Benandonner. When he saw the size of his rival, however, Finn reacted rather curiously : he returned home and dressed himself in baby clothes. When Benandonner came banging on the front door, Finn's wife told him that her husband was out, but made sure to show off her new 'baby'. After seeing the size of the 'child', Benandonner fled, tearing up the causeway as he went, leaving only the remains which can still be seen today.

The tee shot on Finn MacCool's Pitch offers the longer hitters a chance "to go for it". Depending on the weather conditions, the green is reachable but many have tried and failed, wishing that they had taken the conservative approach. Whatever you decide, the hook shot should be left in the bag at all times unless you happen to be carrying climbing equipment.

Gale force winds from the Atlantic are a common feature on this hole, and stormy conditions have contributed to many tragedies over the years, the worst being in 1588 when the Girona, a Spanish cruise ship forming part of a golfing armada, went down within sight of the green.

DOWNPATRICK HEAD GOLF CLUB
10th : DOONBRISTY
176 yards

This extremely tricky par three shares its name with the stack which stands in lofty isolation, only a medium iron shot away from the cliff tops of Downpatrick Head.

The player faces such a challenge when he tees up on Doonbristy that the flag is traditionally flown at half mast as a mark of respect to all the great scores that might have been made had it not been for the intervention of this hole.

Even the walk to the tee is not without its hazards. Players must risk a soaking as they negotiate one of the many puffing holes that are to be found on the cliff tops in this part of Mayo. The holes run down through the rock until they connect with a sea cave below. As the waves crash against the cliff face, a tall plume of water emerges from the puffing hole, making umbrellas the order of the day even when the sun is shining. Not many courses can boast a *vertical* water hazard.

All golf courses, however, tend to suffer from bottle necks which cause slow play. At Downpatrick Head, Doonbristy is particularly prone to this problem, although many members enjoy the entertainment value of watching others having a go.

Suggestions are always forthcoming about how to combat the delays, but the only action taken to date is a ban on all visiting societies, with the exception of firemen and window cleaners.

BEN BULBEN GOLF CLUB
11th : DIARMUID'S DEMISE
565 yards par 5

This county Sligo club enjoys an unrivalled location, on and around Ben Bulben, Ireland's answer to Ayer's Rock in Australia and Table Mountain in South Africa.

The hole is named after the Irish warrior, Diarmuid Ua Duibhne, who was mortally wounded by a magic boar while out hunting on the mountain. Diarmuid was left to die by his rival Fionn MacCumhail who was still embittered by Diarmuid's elopement, many years earlier, with the beautiful Grainne, shortly before she was to be married to Fionn. The incident led to the legendary Pursuit of Diarmuid and Grainne which lasted for sixteen years. With Diarmuid out of the way, Fionn eventually succeeded in marrying Grainne.

Diarmuid may have been the first individual to be killed by a boar on a golf course, but many have been bored to death since then, all within the apparently safe confines of the clubhouse.

As you can see, Diarmuid's Demise runs along the very edge of Ben Bulben, and the hook shot, therefore, should be avoided at all costs - unless you have plenty of time and energy to spare. The retrieval of wayward shots at this hole can take so long that it is not unusual for entrants to the Saturday strokeplay competition to end up among the prizes in the Sunday medal.

WICKLOW GOLF AND COUNTRY CLUB
12th : SUGAR LOAF
435 yards par 4

Sugarloaf, which takes its name from the granite-topped mountain in the background, is one of the toughest driving holes in Irish golf.

Viewed from the tee, the narrow fairway appears to be a very elusive target. More often than not, this proves to be the case and, perhaps understandably, members have been known to vent their frustration at times.

The Wicklow club holds the Irish long distance record for club throwing, and Sugar Loaf is a hole where a lot of practice takes place, although it is rather badly designed for these purposes. After missing the fairway with their tee shot, players often fail to find it with their club throwing, and it is by no means unusual for them to retrieve the ball but lose their club.

For the incurables among you, it is good advice, therefore, to throw the club behind you at this hole. You will be compensated for the extra leg work by the time saved searching among the gorse and heather.

For those of you who think that it may be a better idea simply to throw your opponent's clubs, be warned - this course of action can end in all out warfare.

RING OF KERRY GOLF CLUB
13th : BIRD'S EYE
125 yards par 3

Bird's Eye is one of the shortest holes in Irish golf but it can also be one of the most intimidating. Both tee and green, separated only by a short pitch shot, are perched high up on the precipitous Kerry coastline, commanding a superb view of the Skellig Islands which pierce the clear blue waters of the Atlantic Ocean.

What may seem like a straightforward hole on paper can throw down a serious challenge to even the most accomplished players. The wind can be so ferocious that even sober men have sworn that they have seen the green move while playing their tee shot.

Little Skellig, on the left, is off-limits to human visitors but home to a large colony of gannets. Its proximity provides a constant cacophony, not to mention the threat of aerial bombardment, which can disturb even the deepest concentration.

Having found dry land with your tee shot, the most frightening aspect of the hole is, undoubtedly, crossing the rope-bridge from tee to green. Ring of Kerry has not held a strokeplay competition for many years - the last one was won, in stormy conditions, by a local tightrope walker who was the only player to complete the course. Matchplay has been the name of the game ever since, and any player unable to negotiate the rope-bridge must concede Bird's Eye. Lessons on crossing the bridge are available from the club professional, insurance can be taken out with the club secretary, and Dutch courage is available from the bar.

CLARE GOLF AND COUNTRY CLUB
14th : MOHER'S RUIN
237 yards par 3

It is worth travelling to the west of Ireland just to play Moher's Ruin, the finishing hole at Clare, and the most difficult on the course. The hole, which shelters beneath the towering Cliffs of Moher, has become a bit of a tourist attraction in its own right, capturing the attention of curious visitors to the area.

Players arrive on the tee more in hope than in the expectation of finding the green with their tee shot. Christmas and birthdays do not come round often enough for the members here, and even the most generous supply of golf balls can be seriously depleted after completing the course.

Having played Moher's Ruin once too often perhaps, a few members have followed the advice of Bob Hope, and abandoned golf in favour of painting on the basis that it takes fewer strokes. On leaving the green for the last time, one such member, faced with the difficult decision as to what to give his caddie, handed over his clubs.

The cliff-top building is O'Brien's Tower, built in 1835 as an observation post. It is said that you have more chance of seeing New York from here than a birdie on Moher's Ruin.

Should the day ever dawn, however, when you are faced with a putt for birdie at this hole, it pays to remember two things. Firstly, the green is lightning fast - an aggressive putt means a lost ball - and secondly, under no circumstances walk backwards when lining up your putt.

JURASSIC GOLF AND COUNTRY CLUB
15th : DOLMEN
325 yards par 4

Jurassic is Ireland's oldest club and some would argue that it still includes many fossils, and even the occasional dinosaur, among its members. Dolmen is the newest hole on the course, being added sometime around the year 2500 BC.

Although it is a relatively short par four, Dolmen is a hole with many distinguishing features. The driver must be left in the bag as the steep incline in front of the tee demands the selection of an iron club. Positioning is critical in order to avoid a blind second shot, and only a brave tee shot up the right hand side of the fairway will be rewarded with a glimpse of the green.

The approach shot requires equal measures of nerve and local knowledge, and any shot failing to find the green is deemed to be out of bounds.

Players travelling light, or those who have invested in a caddie, will benefit from their foresight during their descent to the green. In the event of accidents, a first aid box and emergency telephone are available at the entrance to the tunnel which leads to the next hole.

Having negotiated the difficult route from tee to green, there is still a lot of golf to be played. In fact, it was the steep and treacherous nature of this very putting surface that inspired Mark Twain to point out that it is bad sportsmanship to pick up lost balls while they are still rolling.

MULLAGHMORE GOLF CLUB
16th : ROCKY HORROR
412 yards par 4

The course at Mullaghmore sits on the edge of an area known as the Burren, a plateau of limestone and shale covering approximately one hundred square miles of north-west Clare. The name comes from the Gaelic word, b*oireann*, meaning rocky place.

This part of Ireland departs from the traditional image of the 'emerald isle' - it is a harsh place, almost lunar in appearance, and barely able to support human habitation. It was summed up by Cromwell's surveyor as "a savage land, yielding neither water enough to drown a man, nor a tree to hang him, nor soil enough to bury".

The course has been designed in the face of this adversity, although turf has been brought in to make the greens. Fairways, however, remain a scarce resource and taking divots is frowned upon, although the chance very rarely arises. Course overcrowding is virtually unknown, although this has a lot to do with the high rate of wrist injuries sustained by the members.

From the deeds of Oliver Cromwell to the ravages of the potato famine, history lessons are not easily forgotten in these parts, yet, where Rocky Horror is concerned, a great long-term memory is essential if you are to remember your good shots. On the other hand, a very poor short-term memory will help you to forget your many bad ones.

CAUSEWAY COAST
GOLF AND COUNTRY CLUB
17th : THE GIANT'S ORGAN
235 yards par 3

For those of you who are not musically minded, the Giant's Organ gets its name from the striking resemblance between the rock formation to the left of the green and the musical instrument.

With the wind blowing from off the sea, an occasional note can be heard emanating from the rock face. Certain members even claim to have heard hymn music at this spot early one Sunday morning, but the phenomenon may have been linked closely to their drinking habits the night before.

The hole is the second to be featured from the Causeway Golf and Country Club which is situated on and around the Giant's Causeway on the Antrim coastline. Despite what you may read elsewhere, the causeway was built in order to give the Scots easier access to the superior golf and whiskey that Ireland has to offer.

Many a scorecard has been ruined by difficulties encountered at Giant's Organ, but the recent addition of the bunker below the green has been welcomed by all, especially the shorter hitters who now have an outside chance of making par.

Should you find despair at this hole, however, you would do well to remember that a bad day on the golf course will normally beat a good day at the office.

LAKES OF KILLARNEY GOLF CLUB
18th : PANORAMA
465 yards par 4

As it weaves its way between the lakes of Killarney and the mountains of MacGillycuddy's Reeks, there are few courses to rival the beauty of this one, yet part of the splendour was created a long time ago by an act of neglect on the part of a local peasant girl.

The lakes were formed after the young girl forgot to seal the entrance to an enchanted fountain. Having arranged to meet her loved one there, she was lulled to sleep by the music of its flow. By the time the couple awoke, it was too late, and they were drowned by the rising water.

The lake-side fairway on Panorama is relatively generous in its welcome for the tee shot but narrows sharply as it turns towards the green. Although many balls are lost on this hole, the group behind rarely accepts an invitation to play through, most players preferring to savour the view for a little while longer.

The great American golfer, Walter Hagen, shared this philosophy and expressed it thus while playing the hole : "Never hurry and don't worry. You're just here for a short time, so don't forget to stop and smell the flowers on the way."

PLAYABLE AT ALL GOLF CLUBS
19th : THE CRACK
As Long And As Many As You Like

A truly unique hole, yet the nineteenth can be found at every club in Ireland. it is a place to sit and review, sometimes revise, the events of the previous eighteen holes before moving on to lesser matters such as putting the world to rights.

No matter how many over par you are when you arrive at the nineteenth, care should be taken that you do not end up below par by the time you leave. It is a hole which can elicit an unquenchable thirst in some, where the favourite drink of many is their next one.

The nineteenth is the only hole in golf where you can throw away the textbook, forget about keeping your left arm straight and concentrate instead on keeping your right arm bent. For this reason, a few of the members prefer to miss out the first eighteen holes, and go straight to the nineteenth instead.

Although the hole can take a long time to complete, it is usually played with considerable gusto, especially in Ireland where defensive play tends to give way to attacking flair. At the end of it all, however, you are sure to feel relaxed, but remember not to relax too much or you may have to be carried home.